INTRODUCTION TO
DRAWING
A STEP BY STEP GUIDE
BY JOHN HENN

NEW
BURLINGTON
BOOKS

A QUINTET BOOK

ISBN: 1-85348-707-4

This edition was designed and produced by
Quintet Publishing Limited

Jacket Design: Nik Morley

Typeset in Great Britain by
Central Southern Typesetters, Eastbourne
Manufactured in China by
Regent Publishing Services Ltd.

Published by New Burlington Books
6, Blundell Street
London N7 9BH

Contents

Drawing with Pencils, Pastels and Pen & Ink

Jean August Ingres, 'Pencil Study'. Ingres was extremely adept at simple pencil studies of this sort. Using only a rough outline and areas of shading, Ingres captured his subject with economy.

The idea conjured up by the word 'drawing' is invariably of pencil marks made on a sheet of white paper. 'Pencil', therefore, is synonymous with drawing in most peoples' minds. That this should be so, although not by any means entirely true, is understandable. For many years pencil has been found to be the most sympathetic and subtly variable instrument for documenting, describing and analysing an image.

The Italian masters of the 15th century were all familiar with silverpoint, a stick of silver sharpened to a point. Silverpoint was used to enable the artist to build up a continuous tone of great sensitivity. In the past, silverpoint drawing was done on a specially prepared sheet of coloured paper.

Chalk was also a forerunner of the present day pencil and had greater immediacy and fluency than the quieter quality of silverpoint. Most chalk studies were the raw material for subsequent paintings. Indeed, these studies often remained in a master's studio for years, being used in several works and often inherited by students for use in later pictures.

Silverpoint was suitable for deliberate and careful investigation while chalk increased the range of activity.

With chalk the outlines of a proposed composition and the perspective necessary to locate figures within the implied space could be worked out.

Pencil types and supports

Attention should be paid to the broad range of marks available with the pencil from the fine incisive line of a hard lead, to the thick crumbling smudges created by a heavy black lead. Pencils are produced in varying degrees of hardness and a grading system is employed by manufacturers to identify these grades. The 'H' series

are the hardest and the range progresses down to the 8B – an extremely soft lead. The combination of different grades of mark within one picture is very effective, as in the combination of detailing with a 4H to broad, richly rendered and freely applied tones with a 4 or 6B.

The range of pencil types does not end there; wax pencils, charcoal pencils, conté crayons and several others all have their own unique qualities to exploit, combine, and experiment with.

The support used for working in

Edgar Degas, 'Woman Drying Herself'. Degas was one of the great innovators and promoters of pastels. He experimented widely with different techniques and developed a 'painting' method which involved spraying the pastel surface with warm water or milk. Degas' use of gesture and colour are important aspects to study. He was also one of the first artists to use broken colour – strokes of pure colour which 'mix' optically. Many of the Impressionists incorporated his discoveries in their work.

pencil is very important since the quality of the drawing will always be dependent upon the texture and tone of the paper or board used. A hard pencil will make a strong dark line on a rough textured paper, just as a soft lead will make a fine and crisp line on a smoother surface.

Drawing techniques and mixed media
The smudge, and tones comprising linear marks rather like those described in the comments on silverpoint drawing, are all part of the range of techniques possible with the pencil.

The pencil is very effective when used in combination with other media – both water and oil based – and can be drawn on to canvas and gesso grounds, as well as paper. A relatively recent development worth exploiting are coloured pencils. Used either as full colour to describe things as seen, or to introduce colour suggestions into a pencil drawing, they are equally effective. Coloured pencils are also likely to be affected by the texture of

the paper and so the issue of scale is obviously important.

The drawing process
A sound way to learn to render the form and volume in, say, a figure study, is to work in a pencil with a very hard lead on a large, smoothish piece of paper. By this means, if the paper measures about 20in × 30in (50cm × 65cm), the amount of labour needed to make the marks of, say, a 2H pencil show on the surface, allows the artist to scratch away and correct mistakes without the faults needing the use of an eraser. If erasing can be avoided, one can learn from these corrections, for by seeing the 'false' lines left alongside their more accurate brethren, fewer uncertainties should occur.

Pastels

Pastels share some of the characteristics of both painting and drawing media. The sticks, made from finely

powdered pigment and a surprisingly small amount of gum or resin, have been in use for many years. They produce a characteristic powdery quality, which many artists find extremely attractive.

Because the great majority of pastels have an opaque nature, the papers and boards commonly used with them tend to be toned or coloured. Many artists prefer to tone their own surfaces, particularly if textured ones are being used. Their use is often combined with charcoal or black chalk; the latter are harder and so introduce a tough, energetic linear quality, which contrasts well with the soft, blended feeling generally associated with the pure pastel.

Techniques
By experimenting with the widest possible range of marks, surfaces, and techniques, it will become apparent that there is an optimum size, style and feeling for working in pastel. A warm, hot, or cool-toned paper

5

or board, for instance, will produce an entirely different mood and spirit in the eventual work. Roughly applying pastel to coarse paper, or finely smoothing pastels to a fine surface, will have similarly differing effects.

One method of working is to use pastel to render the subject to a highly finished state and then to flood water or milk across the surface. This melts the tones together to form a 'painted' finished picture. The technique was employed by Edgar Degas (1834–1917) and others. Degas used pastel throughout his life to produce some of his most celebrated works. From the briefest of sketches to formal compositions, he was a master of the medium.

Another popular and successful method of working in pastel is a technique known as 'working the lights'. In this, the main structures and features of the painting are ticked in on a toned ground in soft pencil and then the light tones and colours are carefully defined, using light pastels. These will be later developed into the middle and dark tones; here, a torchon, a roll of paper used to blend colours together, can be extremely useful.

A knowledge of 'gesture' is as important in pastel as in all other media. As defined in art practice, gesture means the type of marks made by the individual artist on the surface. The gesture can be long and lingering or short and staccato, depending on the medium, the size of the subject, and the subject matter itself. Experience is the key factor; in pastel, the stroke of the broad side of the stick or the softened finger-rubbed mark will both contribute to the quality of the image. The trick is knowing when to use which technique.

Oil pastel

The oil pastel is a relatively recent innovation. This is a stick of colour, similar to the traditional pastel, but instead consisting of oil-bound pigment in a solid form. It behaves in a very different way to orthodox pastels and should be exploited for its own distinct characteristics.

Since oil pastels are inclined to be more clumsy than 'pure' pastel, it is best to use them on a small scale. The images they produce are fluid and malleable and, as an ingredient in mixed media painting, they have proved themselves able to create a wide range of effects. One technique is to lay in the broad, general outlines of composition and colour harmonies in oil pastel and then overpaint in gouache. If the oil rejects the gouache, a little soft soap can be added to the paint to enable it to cover the pastels effectively.

An attractive result can be achieved from a technique based upon an old method called 'wash off'. Lay in the broad basic composition and block in the main colours with oil pastels. Work up details in coloured inks and gouache, leaving occasional gaps between the features within the piece. When dry, cover the whole work with a coat of white gouache, applying this thickly enough to create a solid sheet of colour.

Carefully spread a further coat of black waterproof India ink over the gouache and allow it to dry completely. Beneath the resulting black surface will be the original design waiting to be revealed. By scraping across the black, inked surface with the flat of a single-edged razor blade, or a similar sharp instrument, the layers beneath will emerge in varying degrees.

Pen and ink

There is a long tradition of pen and ink drawing, its particular incisiveness being found useful for recording fine detail. The studies for the major works executed by Michelangelo and others include a number of pen and ink studies.

With the invention of photo-mechanical methods of printing, the pen and ink drawing has taken on a completely new significance, and we now live in the long shadow of its influence. For the first time, pen and ink is no longer being used for the planning of larger and more significant work, but is used to create the finished work itself.

Prior to the invention of photo-mechanical printing, the draughtsman drew the image on to wooden blocks. These were then engraved by superlative craftsmen so well that the resultant woodblock, ready for printing in the books and magazines of the time, almost totally simulated the character of the original drawing. However, because of the timely and costly process of engraving in this way and the necessarily static feeling imparted to the finished work, it was difficult to transmit the calligraphic feel in the original drawing.

Much finer lines, with closer interstices are possible than those seen in such results; melting the edges of lines by drawing on to dampened paper, rubbing the still wet ink to contrast with the sharper drawn lines will create and suggest further possibilities.

Pen types and supports

Pens are made in a wide variety of

Honoré Daumier, 'The Wayside Railway Station'. Daumier's pictures are unique in their ability to evoke atmosphere and mood. He often used the working classes as subjects for his paintings and drawings.

Michelangelo Buonarotti, 'Studies'. The pen and ink studies of Michelangelo are an excellent way for the artist to study the use of line to create tone and structure.

it back and draw in a small portion over the pencil marks in pen and ink. Follow this by again folding the top sheet down on to the absorbent paper and rub gently over the back in the location of the freshly drawn ink marks, thus transferring it in reverse on to the other surface. Continue this process through until the whole image is transferred.

This technique is of interest not only in its own right but also in combination with others. Traditionally, pen and ink has been used in association with washes of diluted inks and line reinforcing broad masses of simple tones. Splattering tone across and into dry and wet pen and ink lines is one technique, and the use of masking devices to prevent them is another.

Coloured inks
As in the case of coloured pencils, the range of coloured inks is now a part of the artist's repertoire, and a relatively recent phenomena. If used as part of a technique including black and white, these inks are interesting; however, attention should be drawn to the extremely fugitive nature of the colour and their tendency to fade with time. Because of this, it is preferable to avoid combining coloured inks into pictures to be considered otherwise permanent

Mixed media
Whether hatching finely or running lines freely over the page, pen and ink will respond in a great many ways. Mixed with other media, a good deal of invention can take place with coloured or black ink on coloured grounds; or black lines on a carefully rendered watercolour will bring forth fresh results. Combine several types of nib and brush marks. Don't forget the newer types of pen such as the rapidograph and ballpoint pens.

Erasing
To erase false marks, make sure the ink is dry and scrape gently with a knife or razor to remove the unsuccessful area. By carefully burnishing the erased area, one can render the surface suitable for redrawing.

Composition

The illustrations created by perspective systems are a major factor in constructing a good, sound composition. Composition is the term used to express organization of varied and

sizes and styles and the supports suitable are of great number. From mapping pens – extremely fine nibs developed for cartographers – to coarse steel, inflexible nibs and variations in between, all are readily available. The making of pens from quills and reeds is well worth persevering with, and varying the size of the nib will result in a great number of variations. Making use of unlikely sources for nibs is not to be discounted. Those made for use in lettering will make a mark fatter, fuller, and more flowing than most of the standard types. Again, the paper used will affect the appearance of the finished piece of work.

The range of supports does not necessarily stop with those available from the artists' supplier. Absorbent surfaces – those treated with size – are sympathetic upon which to make certain images. Wrapping paper, blotting paper and tracing paper take the ink from the pen in entirely different ways.

Techniques
An interesting result can be achieved by making drawings by means of the offset technique. On a sheet of highly sized paper – tracing paper or similar – tick in the main points of the drawing and bring it to a finished stage with pencils. When you consider the picture ready for transfer, hinge the sheet of paper along the long edge to a sheet of blotting or semi-absorbent paper with adhesive tape. Make sure that the original drawing can be folded flat to present the entire drawing image neatly on to the other sheet. Then fold

disparate elements within the painting to create legibility and visual interest. The balance and interrelationship of lines, masses, colours, and movement are also aspects of composition.

Over the centuries, the attempt to create standards for the making of art has taken many forms from ideal proportions for drawing the human form, to systematic colour patterning.

The 'ideal', as exemplified by the Greeks as the definition of perfect proportion, was based upon a theory known as the Golden Section. This is a mathematical formula by which a line is divided in such a way that the smaller part is to the larger as the larger part is to the whole. The Golden Section was considered to hold balance naturally, entirely satisfying the human eye for symmetry and harmony. Ever since this rule was proposed, geometry has been an important and recurring concept in painting and drawing.

Atmosphere can only be sustained over the whole surface by equal consideration being given to its several parts. The basic types of composition are those based on geometry which have been used for a great many years, both in the simple and more sophisticated forms. For example, often the triangular structure found in early Madonna and Child paintings will be complemented by an inverted or interrelated triangle, sometimes to an astonishingly complex degree.

Piero della Francesca (1410/20–1492) was an Italian artist as interested in mathematics as in art but the complicated compositional structures he used did not detract from the picture's beauty and compassion. Piero is considered one of the world's greatest masters and little effort is needed to see why – not only are the linear interrelationships on the picture surface highly resolved, but colour is used both logically and to enhance the aims and intentions of the picture.

These compositions are distinguished by a generally static and classical mood – an inevitable outcome of the systems used. Alternative methods have long been used and the rhythmic composition of a Rubens or Delacroix show some of them in action. In order to suggest movement, or to lead the eye across the picture surface, it is necessary to achieve balance by some other means. The interlocking of the main directional lines into a satisfactory arrangement to tell

 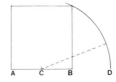  

The Golden Section. This rule is ascribed to Euclid as the ideal division of a surface. Far left: To find the vertical Section, divide line AB in half to create C. Next, draw a radius from the top right corner to create D. In the next picture, draw in lines to create a rectangle. Point BG is the vertical Section. Far right: To find the horizontal Section, draw a line from the top of the vertical line G to the bottom right corner. Create a radius from the top right corner downward. Where the line and arc intersect is the horizontal Section.

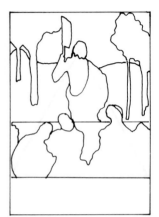

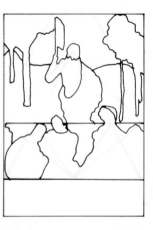

Structure. The 15th century Italian artist Piero della Francesca was as interested in geometry as in painting. Top right: The triangle is the geometric base from which Piero worked. Bottom right: Following this principle, many triangles, can be discovered.

the story use the surface and employ all available space.

The picture space

How often has one seen pictures with the interest focused in the centre, leaving corners and outer edges unoccupied, or localized nests of activity with barren and uninteresting deserts of space all around? Poussin, (1594–1665) the French painter, was greatly concerned with the grammar of composition and would invite the viewer to gain by viewing beyond the focal point all parts of the canvas being used.

Dramatic gesture demands balance of an asymmetrical kind. The eye needs to make space for such implied movement, in much the same way that a profile portrait will require more space between the front of the face and edge, than between the back and parallel edges.

Dramatic impact will be enhanced within the composition by a variety in scale and to this end the exploitation of close and distant viewing, not only tonally as in atmospheric perspective, but as contrasts of size on the surface. The eye of a head in close up will be seen to be approximately the same size as the full figure at a short distance behind. A sea gull in flight above foreground cliffs will occupy the major part of the picture plane. Exploit these contrasts and use them with the other useful contributory parts.

Perspective

What is a good picture? There is no simple answer; perhaps one that excites or disturbs, not one necessarily pleasing to the eye, but containing a great deal of visual interest. Not only should the artist be facile in his knowledge and use of the materials, but he or she should be conversant with these other important ingredients of visual communication and, through the fusion of these various elements, achieve his or her ambitions.

In picture making, the elements every artist needs to understand in order to best exploit them include colour, composition, and perspective. The fusion of these components with a good basic drawing ability and sound technique give the artist an opportunity to express his personal vision.

One, two, and three point perspective. When two planes are visible, the parallel lines converge at a single vanishing point. When three planes are visible, two points are required. If a cube is seen above or below the horizon line, three points are used.

Seeing. The human eye functions in a highly complex system allowing us to view the world in three dimensions. Distance is formulated by the angle of convergence of the image on the retina. When many objects are viewed, sophisticated computations take place in the brain.

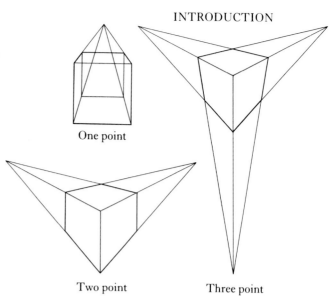

One point

Two point

Three point

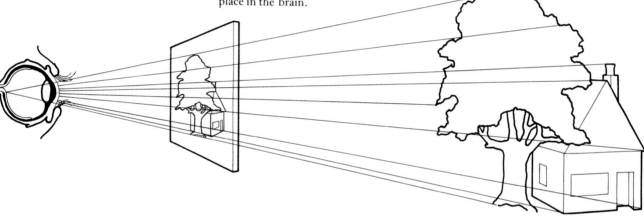

Pieter Bruegel, 'The Fall of Icarus'. The concept of aerial perspective is clearly shown in this painting. Notice how objects close up are precise and detailed and those in the middle and far distance become hazy and less well defined.

9

Pen and ink

FINE, LINEAR DRAWING with pen and ink requires a careful, deliberate approach. Tonal shading must be developed gradually and crosshatching cannot be rapidly blocked in. The crisp, emphatic lines of a pen drawing have no equivalent and it is worthwhile to acquire the skill and patience to handle the pen to produce the dramatic, graphic effects of this medium.

This drawing gives a general impression of a landscape by starting with a loose sketch which outlines shapes and positions of trees and bushes. Each area of hatched lines and irregular, scribbled marks correspond to the basic tonal and textural structure. While the elements are treated separately, the whole image is constantly considered as a whole and brought together in the final stages.

Your technique should be controlled but not rigid – keep the pen well charged with ink and make decisive, fluid strokes. Even if the drawing is quite small, the marks should be as vigorous as possible, since it is texture, not colour, which provides visual interest.

Materials

Surface
Thick white cartridge paper

Size
12in × 8in (30cm × 20cm)

Tools
HB pencil
Dip pen
Medium nib

Colours
Black waterproof India ink

1. Make a light sketch of the layout with an HB pencil. Start to draw with the pen showing rough outlines and tones.

2. Develop the tones using the large tree as a focal point and working outwards. Build up the texture with fluid scribbled marks and crisp lines.

Crosshatching tones

3. Work across the paper sketching in shapes and elaborating forms.

4. Extend the hatched tones, establishing receding planes and overall shape of the image. Develop details in the foreground with small, irregular patterns.

5. Concentrate on details, particularly in the foreground, and work over the outlines of the shapes to soften the contours.

This detail of the shadow area behind the tree shows the artist using crosshatching to develop dense and varied tonal areas.

Pastel

WHILE PASTELS are generally considered a drawing medium, working with them involves both painting and drawing skills. The same principles apply to pastels as to many painting media as seen in the overlaying of colours to create new colours and transparency.

The main difference between using pastel and the usual painting media is that the former cannot be easily erased or corrected. The artist's only recourse to correcting a pastel drawing is to overlay more colour. For this reason the picture should be developed through careful and well thought-out layering of tone and colour rather than through heavy and dense application of the pastels.

In this picture the artist has used some elements of the pointillist technique without the use of 'points'. Rather, thin strokes of pure colour have been laid down beside and on top of one another to give the impression of mixing colours and tones. The picture is based primarily on the use of warm and cool colours – red and blue – and their interraction with one another. By careful use of complementary colours, such as a touch of a reddish tone in a predominantly blue area, a dull and predictable picture is avoided. Close examination of the finished picture reveals that where there is a large area of one colour – blue for example – its complement, red, has been added to give the picture unity. The complementary colour also 'bounces off' the other warm colour areas, unifying the picture as a whole.

Materials

Surface
Heavy weight pastel paper

Size
18.5in × 26in (46cm × 65cm)

Tools
Willow charcoal
Rags or tissues
Fixative

Colours

Blue-green	Light red
Cobalt blue	Light yellow
Crimson	Orange
Dark blue	Pale blue
Dark green	Yellow

1. With broad strokes, lay in the basic warm and cool colours as an underpainting.

2. With heavier, linear strokes, begin to develop darker tones of these general colour areas moving over the paper with one colour at a time.

3. Begin to lay in lighter, warmer tones of orange, yellow, and red building up the colour contrasts of the warm-cool, blue-red motif. Keep the strokes light.

4. Return to the dark colours previously used, heightening shadow areas with a heavier stroke.

5. With cobalt blue, lighten any areas which appear too heavy or dark. Put in the sky with pale blue.

6. Return to the dark blue, red, and green colours to put in the final touches of emphasis and contrast using stroke to give direction and shape.

Overlaying pure colour

With pastel, the artist produces colours which mix optically on the surface by applying thin lines of pure colour one over the other. Here, pale blue strokes are laid over crimson in the wall to create purple.

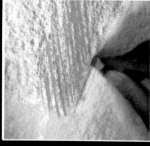

Pencil

WASH AND LINE illustrates the ability of mixed media to capture an image both simply and directly. By a skilfull use of line and carefully placed touches of wash, the artist is able to reduce the subject to its bare essentials, creating a picture which is fresh and simple in style.

How to decide upon the ratio of line to wash, and vice versa, takes practice and a keen eye. There are no hard and fast rules but, in general, it is best to keep the image as clear and uncluttered as possible. The temptation to cover the surface with many colours and techniques is a common one; it takes practice, restraint, and a critical eye to put into the picture only what is absolutely essential to best express the subject.

A good reason for resisting the temptation to cover the page is that often the plain white surface can emphasize a line or dab of colour far more than any techniques or additional colours can. It is the use of contrast – the broad white or tinted paper contrasting with the sharp edge of a line or subtle wash of colour – which serves to emphasize and draw attention to the image. The emptiness and cleanness of a few well-chosen lines and dots of colour, when combined with the untouched surface can create an image of eye-catching simplicity.

Materials

<u>Surface</u>
Thick cartridge paper

<u>Size</u>
26in × 18in (65cm × 45cm)

<u>Tools</u>
4B pencil
Putty rubber

<u>Colours</u>
Gold ochre watercolour

<u>Medium</u>
Water

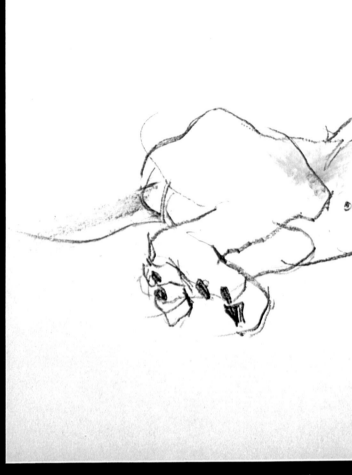

The final touches of detail are put in with a soft, dark pencil.

1. Begin by putting a small amount of gold ochre directly on to a small piece of rag.

2. Rub the gold ochre on to the surface to create general colour areas. Use your finger or fingers to draw with the paint and create feathered textures similar to fur.

Feathering · drawing in shapes · details

With a dense stroke, the artist is here seen working over the yellow wash to put in the general shape of the lion.

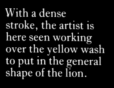

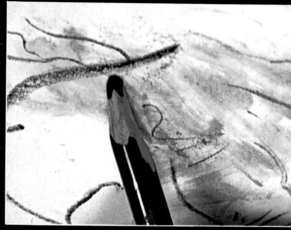

A feathered texture can be achieved by using the fingers to lightly touch the paint on to the surface. Do not use too much paint on the rag and do not dilute with turpentine.

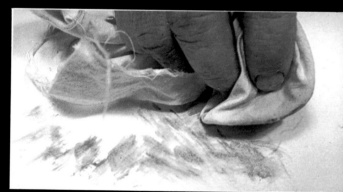

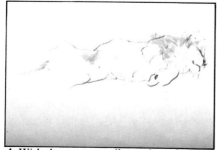

3. With a soft, dark pencil, begin to describe the lion's head over the gold ochre paint. Vary the thickness and width of the line.

4. With the same pencil, continue down the body of the lion with a light, flowing stroke.

5. Reinforce outlines with more pressure. Put in dark details in the head and feet.

Pen and ink

THE LOOSE LINE and confident strokes which experienced pen and ink artists achieve are acquired more by a relaxed attitude than superior drawing talents. More than any other medium, if the artist is worried about his strokes, the pen and ink drawing will immediately reveal his concern; the artist must make a conscious effort to overcome a desire to control or inhibit the line of the pen and the flow of the ink.

The artist has here achieved an informal sketch with little detail or careful rendering. The strokes are loose, flowing, casual. While there are many artists who consider any form of correction wrong, it is perfectly acceptable to correct a pen and ink drawing, as the artist has done here, with white gouache. On the other hand, as it is impossible to draw over lumps of white paint without interrupting the flow of the line, massive correcting may destroy the naturalness of the picture.

Materials

Surface
Smooth cartridge paper

Size
6.5in × 9in (16cm × 22cm)

Tools
2B pencil
Dip pen
Medium nib
No 2 sable brush

Colours
Black waterproof India ink
White designer's gouache

Medium
Water

1. With a 2B pencil, roughly sketch in the horse's head and area to be worked within.

2. Develop the eyes with fine crosshatching. If any area of the drawing becomes too dense, it may be corrected with a small sable brush and gouache.

3. Work down the head indicating musculature with a light, diagonal stroke.

4. Block in the surrounding area with broad, dark strokes. To create a darker tone, work back over these strokes in another direction.

5. Put in the darkest areas with a scribbling motion and plenty of ink. Redefine the outlines of the head with a dense, dark line.

6. Work back into the head and surrounding area with crosshatching to create darker tones and shadow areas.

Beginning details · correcting

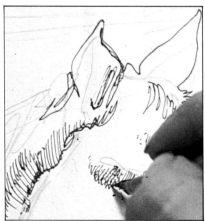

With a very fine nib, the artist puts in details around the eye.

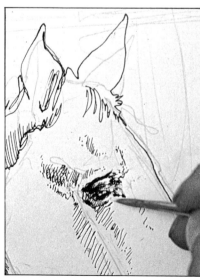

Small areas of ink can be corrected by using a small brush and white designers' gouache. This can be used for small corrections only.

Pastel

IN TERMS OF colour, shape, and gesture, the subject for this picture is well suited to a pastel drawing as bold colours and sharp, gestural strokes are few of the many potential uses of pastel. Of course the technique used will determine the end result; if this picture had been executed with heavy blending, smudging and subtle colour the results would be quite different.

The colours used are basically complementary: red, orange and pink; blue, purple and green. It is worth remembering that colour is created by light, and colour will always reflect and bounce off neighbouring colours. The artist has exploited this by using a complementary colour within a predominant colour area. Thus there are touches of red in the purple flowers, and touches of purple in the red and orange flowers. The dark blue used to describe the stems and shadow areas works as a contrast to both the purple, blue, and red, intensifying and adding depth to the overall picture.

The composition was purposely arranged to give a feeling of closeness. The white of the paper works in stark contrast to the densely clustered stems and flowers in the bottom left corner and the directional strokes serve to lead the eye upward and across the page.

Materials

Surface
Pastel paper

Size
16in × 20in (40cm × 50cm)

Tools
Tissue or rag
Willow charcoal
Fixative

Colours

Blue-green	Orange
Cadmium red medium	Pale blue
Cadmium yellow medium	Pink
Cobalt blue	Prussian blue
Dark green	White
Light green	

1. After roughing in the flower shapes with charcoal, lightly sketch in the flowers in pink, red, and purple and the stems in light and dark greens.

2. With a small piece of tissue, blend the colour tones of the flowers. With pale blue, work back into the purple flowers describing the petals with sharp strokes.

A method of blending is to use a small piece of tissue. Unlike a finger, the tissue will both blend colours and pick up the pastel, thus lightening the tone.

Pastel marks can either be left as clean strokes or blended into subtle gradations of tone and colour. Here the artist is blending within the flowers, mixing the orange and pink.

Using the tip of a pastel, the artist describes stem and leaf shapes with a quick, loose motion.

3. With cadmium red and orange, emphasize the petal shapes with sharp strokes. With dark blue, define stems with the same sharp, directional strokes.

4. With purple pastel, put a heavier layer down within the blue flowers. Use the same colour to put in additional leaf and stem shapes with a loose stroke.

5. Returning to the flowers, apply deeper tones with more pressure. Add touches of red to the purple flowers. Create flower centres with yellow in the pink flowers.

Finished picture blending · stem and leaf shapes

To finish the picture (<u>right</u>), the artist continued to develop strong dark areas with blue. As a final step, a tissue was used to pick up loose colour and blend into the right hand corner.

PERFECTING THE techniques needed to draw effectively in pastel takes time. As pastels are loose and powdery, the sticks must be carefully manipulated to achieve any degree of precision. If you work on tinted paper, the light tones may be handled as positive, strong colours while the tint adds depth to the overall tone of the work.

Outlines, where used, should be light and sketchy, merely providing a guideline to be eventually overlaid by areas of colour. Spray the drawing with fixative whenever necessary to keep the colours bright and stable. Overlay layers of colour with light strokes of the pastels to create soft, intermediary tones.

Materials

Surface	
Blue pastel paper	

Size	
11in × 15in (27cm × 37cm)	

Tools	
Fixative	

Colours	
Black	Orange
Cobalt blue	Pink
Dark and light green	White
Dark and light red	Yellow

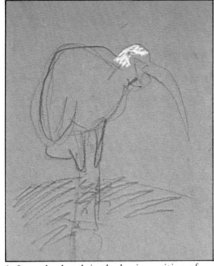

1. Loosely sketch in the basic position of the bird with red and orange pastels. Draw the crest of the head in white.

2. Work over the drawing with vigorous, scribbled marks, contrasting the orange and red of the bird against green and yellow in the background.

3. Construct a solid impression of shape, drawing into the form with white and black. Work into the background with light tones.

4. Strengthen outlines on the bird in black and lay in a dark green behind. Add small details in blue and white.

5. Strengthen the colour over the whole image, showing shadows and highlights. Overlay scribbled patches of different colours.

6. Spray the drawing with fixative and let it dry. Reinforce the red shapes, giving the form more definition. Work up linear details in the background.

Developing general shapes and tones · highlighting

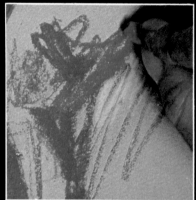

Here the artist begins to block in the colour of the bird with a very loose, scribbling motion.

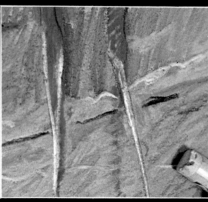

With pale yellow, the artist moves across the picture putting in loose lines of highlight.

Pencil

THIS PICTURE illustrates how willow charcoal, although a fragile medium, can create a very dramatic finished drawing. The drawing process was one of working up dark areas and then modifying them with a putty rubber to achieve a balance between light and shadow. There is a constant movement between the building up of dark areas, lightening them, and then working back into the shadow areas – and then repeating the entire process.

In all drawing media, and particularly with charcoal, it is to your advantage to experiment with the various textures and tones the medium is capable of producing. From a very fine, fluid line to a heavy and dense black, charcoal is flexible enough to fulfil every creative need. Because it is so easily erased, artists feel comfortable with willow charcoal.

Materials

<u>Surface</u>
Cartridge paper

<u>Size</u>
20in × 24in (50cm × 60cm)

<u>Tools</u>
Light and medium willow charcoal
Putty rubber
Tissues
Fixative

1. With the end of a piece of light charcoal, rough in the general shapes. Using the side of the stick, begin to block in the various shadow areas.

3. With a putty rubber, erase out highlight areas in cast and fabric.

5. Work back into the head using the side of a piece of light charcoal. Blend with a piece of rag or a finger.

2. Blend charcoal over the face and draw in the features. Strengthen outlines with a heavy line.

4. With medium charcoal, put in shape and shadows in the fabric and the area around the head. Draw in the outline of the fabric and the table.

6. Blend the background shadow. With the putty rubber, lighten all shadows by lightly drawing the rubber across the surface.

Finished picture · facial details · using a putty rubber

The attractive qualities of using willow charcoal are shown in the finished picture. By a skilful handling of tone and texture, the artist has produced an unusual still life. Note in particular the combination of different textures and shapes to add visual interest.

Here the artist puts in dark facial details using the tip of the charcoal.

By using a putty rubber, the artist can erase back through the charcoal layer to create highlights and subtle tones of grey.

Pen and ink

WHILE IT IS possible to describe a subject with accuracy and precision, a picture often needs some creative licence to make it more interesting. In this case, the artist has taken the general shape, composition, and colour of the subject and through an individual use of line and colour washes has exaggerated features to make the picture more descriptive. The techniques used are washed-in colour, line, and crosshatching, juxtaposed to create an interesting combination of textures.

One important aspect of this drawing is the use of negative space to define details. In the finished picture, the laces outside of the boot have been created by the use of line. Moving on to the boot's surface, it is the area of coloured wash surrounding the white of the paper which continues the image of the lace rather than the pen line itself.

Materials

Surface
Cartridge paper

Size
15in × 22in (38cm × 58cm)

Tools
Pen holder
Small nib
No 2 sable brush
Palette

Ink colours
Black waterproof India ink
Burnt sienna
Red

Medium
Water

1. Begin to put in the outline, varying the line by moving the pen both quickly and slowly. Dip a brush in water and let the pen line bleed into that wet area.

2. Carry the outline further down using red ink. Begin to create shadow textures within the boot with the same red, applied in directional strokes.

3. Mix a small amount of red and burnt sienna and work into the other boot. With pen and black ink, rework the outline of the boot allowing the ink to run .

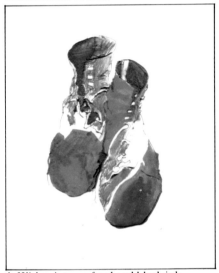

4. With mixture of red and black ink, crosshatch in the remaining white area of the right boot, leaving parts of the surface untouched to create laces and holes.

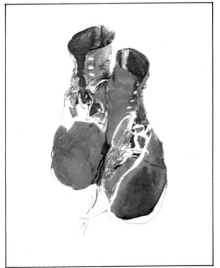

5. Using the pen and black ink, work back into the shoe with crosshatching strokes to create the area around the laces.

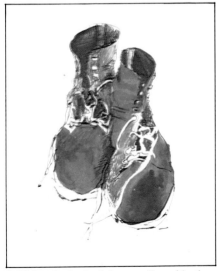

6. Using the back of the pen dipped in the black ink, roughly describe the sole of the boots.

Finished picture · preliminary wash · back of pen · negative space and line

The artist completed the picture by laying a darker wash over shadow areas in the left shoe.

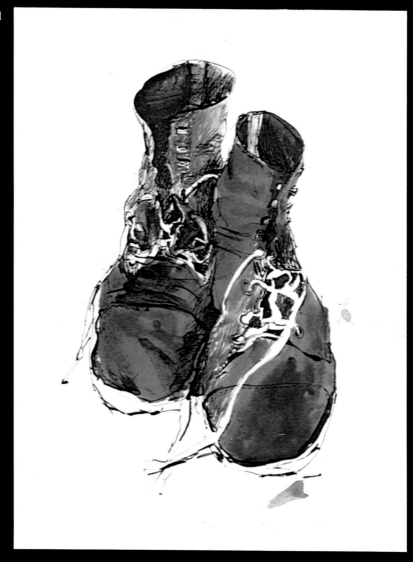

The preliminary wash is put in and will later be worked over with pen and ink.

Using negative space to describe shape, the artist uses a hatched tone to create a white area.

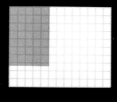

By turning the pen on its back, the artist is able to create a rough, jagged line.

Pastel

THE STILL life can be an excellent way for the artist to explore various media and experiment with different ways of seeing. The choice of objects and their arrangement is virtually infinite; the artist can pick and choose and arrange his subject to suit every need.

In this pastel, the artist chose to work with simple objects and a few bold colours. While this may at first seem the easier course to take – as opposed to complex subject matter and colour schemes – to work with a few primary colours and a simple subject can often be a very difficult task. The main problem in working with bold colours is how to control their intensities so that one does not overpower the other. Although tones and hues may be altered and adjusted by blending, to retain the freshness and vibrancy of the individual colours demands that the artist carefully balance and weigh individual colour areas. One way to ensure a balanced picture is to introduce a complementary colour into a general colour area. Thus in this picture there are small strokes of red within predominantly blue areas, and vice versa. This will also help to give the picture unity, as the observer's eye will pick up the individual colours as it moves around the picture.

Materials

Surface
Pastel paper

Size
18.5in × 26in (46cm × 65cm)

Tools
HB pencil or willow charcoal
Tissues or rags
Fixative

Colours
Blue-green	Pale blue
Cobalt blue	Pink
Deep red	Prussian blue
Green	Yellow
Orange	

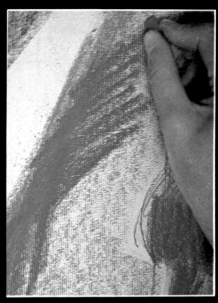

After the initial areas of colour have been laid down, the artist works back over these to strengthen tones.

Overlaying thin strokes of pure colour will create an optical colour mixture on the drawing surface.

1. After lightly sketching the subject in with pencil, use the side of the chalk to put in the main colour areas in blue, green, and orange.

2. Using the end of the chalk, begin to work up stronger colours with sharp, directional strokes.

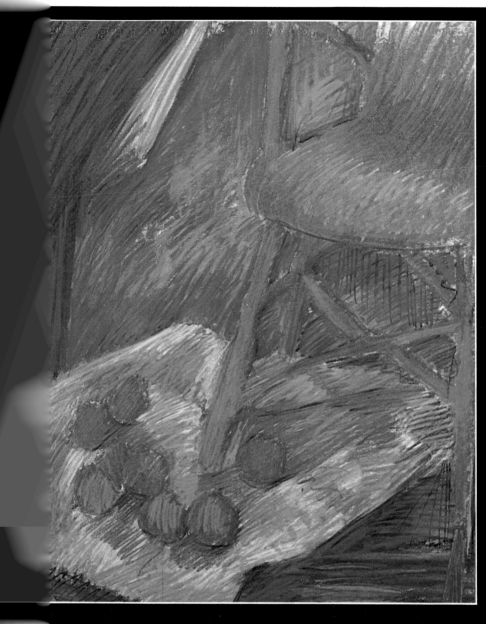

Finished picture · strengthening tones · mixing colour · textures

The finished picture shows a skilful handling of strong primary colours to create a balanced and dynamic image. Compositionally, the use of forceful diagonals adds to the overall vitality of the picture.

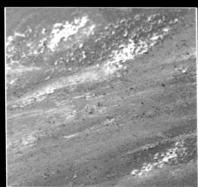

The surface texture is clearly seen in this picture; dense areas of colour are mixed with white gaps in the paper to create a gradated effect.

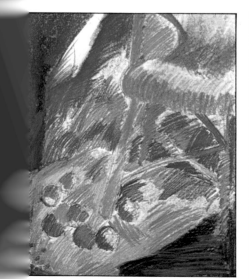

3. Begin to describe lights and darks in green areas by using various tones of green. Carry the red tone into the blue of the backdrop.

4. Intensify dark areas with dark green, Prussian blue, and dark red.

5. With pale blue, work into the foreground area as a highlight and tone down the background with the same colour.

ARTISTS WHO experiment with oil pastels quickly grasp their potential for producing strong, brilliant pictures. They are an extremely flexible medium and can be used either like traditional chalk pastels in thin layers of colour, or painted on to the surface by softening them with turpentine and applying them with a palette knife.

The picture shown here illustrates the intensity and brilliance characteristic of oil pastels in creating an interesting and dramatic picture. They are best suited to bold, colourful work, although it is just as possible to work with subtle overlays of colour. There is a possibility of the surface being built up too quickly, but the artist can always scratch back into the pastel with a sharp tool to either clean up the surface or draw in fine lines of detail.

The composition of this drawing is particularly striking in its use of strong shapes, colours, and the clean white space of the paper. The lack of any additional background information in no way detracts from the forcefulness of the image and, if anything, causes the subject to stand out in bold relief.

Materials

__Surface__
Rough, heavyweight drawing paper

__Size__
21in × 23in (52cm × 57.5cm)

__Tools__
HB pencil

__Colours__
Black	Medium red
Dark blue	Pink
Green	Yellow

1. Lightly sketch in the subject with an HB pencil.

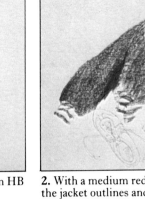

2. With a medium red pastel, work over the jacket outlines and block in red with light, broad strokes.

3. With dark blue, rough in the shadow areas with light strokes.

4. With a medium yellow, put in the trim on the jacket. With the same red as before, put in the red of the shoes. Do the same with a green pastel.

5. With medium yellow, block in the rest of the shoe colour, pressing the pastel hard into the surface.

6. Work back into the jacket with the medium red, bearing hard against the surface. Rework the shadow areas with the same pressure.

7. Continue the previous step until the entire jacket area is covered.

8. Work over the red in the jacket with deep blue, strengthening shadow areas. With a pink pastel, put in highlights in the jacket.

Colour areas · developing the picture

The artist begins
by roughing in the
basic colour areas
using a light,
sweeping motion.

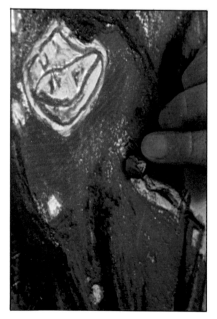

With each
subsequent layer of
colour, the pastel is
pressed more firmly
on to the surface to
fill the tiny white
gaps in the paper
grain.

Pencil

FIGURE DRAWING IN pencil is one of the most useful skills for artists to acquire and is usually included in the first projects given in art schools.

Interesting variations can be obtained by placing the figure in strong light and shadow. If the effect of the light is to be the main interest of the drawing, the picture must be treated as a tonal study by taking advantage of the patterns of light and shade across the forms.

Large areas of pencil shading can become either boring or messy, so the tones must be developed gradually and the textures varied to define separate forms. The dense grey background area in this drawing is built up with layers of fine, criss-crossed marks, loosely woven together to create an overall tone. The shading on the figure is more solid and close-knit, and the dark tones are contrasted with the bare white paper representing the fall of the light.

Materials

Surface
Thick cartridge paper

Size
24in × 16in (60cm × 40cm)

Tools
HB and 2B pencils
Putty rubber
Fixative

1. To establish the scale, start by making a brief outline sketch of the figure. Work into the shape of the head, laying in the darkest tones.

2. Strengthen the outline, working down from the head, and block in dark stripes of shadow cutting across the body. Lay a mid-toned grey behind the head.

Describing tone

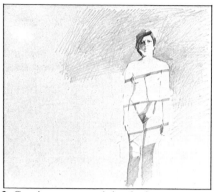

3. Continue to extend the shadow pattern on the figure with dark shading. Develop the background tone, keeping the marks light and loose.

4. Draw into the background behind the figure, lightly outlining shapes with tonal shading.

5. Complete the area of background tone and work back into the shapes of the figure and shadows, building up details in the forms and patterns.

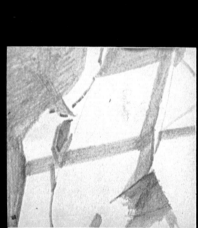

Broad areas of tone are created by using light strokes and consistent pressure. Note that the lines of shadow are not precisely drawn but are irregular and rough.

THE GENERAL impression of this drawing is similar to an old photograph or print due largely to the colour of the paper and the soft pencil tones. The picture shows how pencil can be used with a light, subtle touch to create a peaceful, stable atmosphere.

The effect is also similar to the drawings of the French artist Seurat who, by using rough paper and a soft, dark crayon, was able to create tonal areas duplicating the pointillist technique. A rough surface will lessen the linear effect of the pencil and blend tones more evenly than smooth paper.

The artist here depended upon the use of tone to create an illusion of space and depth and, as seen in the head, this can heighten the overall emphasis of the figure within the picture plane. Although most of the page is blank with no indication of the environment, putting the dark shadow area outside the face gives an impression of depth and space.

Materials

Surface
Pumpkin coloured pastel paper

Size
16in × 20in (40cm × 50cm)

Tools
2B and 4B pencils
Putty rubber
Tissues
Fixative

1. Lightly sketch in the outlines of the figure with a 2B pencil.

2. Begin very lightly to put in the shadow areas with loose, directional strokes. Add dark details around the neck.

3. Work back into the hair with more pressure, building up darks. Strengthen face and chair outlines.

4. Begin to work outside of the face with very light strokes. Carry this over to the flower shape.

5. Strengthen the shadow areas within the figure. With a 2B pencil, work down the figure, roughing in general outlines and shadow areas.

6. With a 4B pencil, strengthen details of face and flower. With same, darken shadow areas in the dress.

Creating tones with putty rubber

The artist works into the facial details using a combination of grey tones and the clean paper surface to describe shadow and highlight areas.

Creating tones with putty rubber

Pen and ink

WHILE PEN AND ink may at first prove uncomfortable and awkward to work with, the artist will soon develop a natural feel for the movement of the pen, the flow of the ink, and which gestures produce which marks. The pen and ink draughtsman creates a drawing from the use of the white of the paper, the black of the ink, and the many tones in between these two. These tones are usually created by the use of individual lines of ink which, when laid over one another in various directions, create a mesh-like effect, giving an impression of shadow and depth. Unlike other drawing and painting media, the pen and ink artist is limited to the use of line for developing tone, but, as demonstrated in this drawing, creating a highly modelled, accurate drawing presents no problem despite this limitation.

In this drawing, the artist, with a minimum of detail, has accurately rendered the figure. The simple use of outline and shaded, crosshatched areas alone gives the figure shape, dimension and weight. The tone created by pen and ink can be very subtly varied and need not have a harsh black and white effect, if carefully graduated and controlled. If you look carefully at the area of the hand resting on the knee, you will see that only loose, rough strokes have been used to describe the shadow areas.

Materials

Surface
Smooth cartridge paper

Size
9in × 12in (22cm × 30cm)

Tools
Dip pen
Fine nib
2B pencil

Colours
Black waterproof ink

1. Sketch in the figure very roughly with a 2B pencil. Put in general outlines in ink and begin to describe shadow areas.

2. Continue the outline of the figure and return to put in shadow areas. Use a hatching stroke to define muscles.

3. Continue outline of the arm. Moving outside of the figure, very loosely put in broad strokes, working in one direction.

4. Continue down to hands and legs of figure, putting in outlines and then working into shadow areas with light strokes.

5. Carry background tone down behind the chair using same directional strokes. Leave white of paper bare to define chair shape.

6. Changing the direction of the line, put in general shadow over the leg. Crosshatch over the background shadow to create a denser tone.

Defining shadow areas

Broad areas of
light hatching are
defined by using a
dark outline to
enclose the strokes.

WHILE A large variety of commercial pens and nibs are available, it is interesting to experiment with hand-cut pens made from quills or hollow sticks. A thick reed pen is used here to give a bold, fluid line to create a spontaneous image.

Drawing with line will give the basic outlines of the forms; the image is then given volume by loose washes of thin, wet colour. A rich surface texture can be built up with this technique so, although only two colours have been used in this picture, a considerable variety of tonal density is achieved.

The intention is not to depict the subject in meticulous detail, but to record a lively impression of the mood and pose which exploits the freedom and diversity of the medium. If the pen is used on dry paper, or over a dry wash it makes a strong, sharp line. When line is applied into wet layers they will spread and feather. Be careful when drawing into a wet area not to tear the damp paper with the point of the pen. Vary the shapes and tones of the washes to provide a contrast between hard-edged shapes and subtly blended tones so that the full versatility of the medium contributes to the overall effect.

Materials

Surface
Stretched cartridge paper

Size
18in × 22in (45cm × 55cm)

Tools
Hollow piece of reed or willow
Knife or scalpel
No 8 round sable brush

Colours
Brown ink
Black waterproof India ink

Medium
Water

1. Dip the pen in black ink diluted with water and draw the profile of the head. Using a small sable brush, apply thin washes of brown ink.

2. Continue to build up the washes, preserving areas of white. Use the pen to define the linear shapes in the foreground and background.

Making the reed pen the pen line

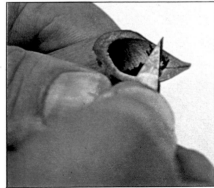

A reed pen can be made from any type of hollow wood. Once roughly shaped, the point is refined with a small knife. The line created by a reed pen is irregular yet soft and produces an effect very suitable for figure work.

3. Lay in broad washes of diluted brown and black inks, working across the entire picture.

4. Draw the figure in more detail using bold, fluid lines. Enrich the shadows with additional washes of brown and black ink.

5. Strengthen linear detail and dark tones with the pen and brush in black.

Pastel

PASTEL drawing requires a combination of drawing and painting skills. It can be treated either as a linear medium for outlines and loosely hatched textures, or the colour may be laid in broad, grainy patches and blended with the fingers or a rag. Pastel colour is soft and powdery and, although it is held together by the tooth of the paper, the surface is always unstable. The drawing should be sprayed with fixative frequently to hold the image while further layers are applied.

The rich textures are built up in a series of overlaid marks, carefully manipulated to describe the forms in terms of their component shapes and colour relationships. In this drawing, the pastel strokes have a vertical emphasis, but sometimes marks follow the direction of the forms in order to emphasize a particular curve or angle. It is easier to control the overall image if the strokes follow one direction. In the initial stages of the drawing use medium soft pastels, graduating to the soft type to develop texture as the drawing progresses.

Materials

Surface
Tinted rag paper

Size
23in × 30in (57cm × 75cm)

Tools
Fixative

Colours
Black	Light yellow
Cobalt blue	Olive green
Dark brown	Red
Flesh	Venetian red
Grey	Ultramarine blue

1. Mark the position of the head and limbs with a pink pastel tint and roughly block in the structure of the figure with pink, light yellow, brown and grey.

2. Work lightly over the whole figure, weaving colours together so basic shapes and tones begin to emerge. Use grey and blue to suggest dark tones.

4. Develop cool tones in the drapery with light blue and white and darken the background colour with broad vertical strokes of olive green and ultramarine.

5. Work over the composition with tones of grey to strengthen shadows. Draw into the figure with light yellow and dark red to build up the solidity of the form.

7. Intensify the blues in the background, laying in brown and green to vary the colour. Develop the colours over the whole drawing, altering if necessary.

8. Emphasize highlights with yellow and white and lighten the background colour with cobalt blue and white. Add touches of warm pink tones into the drapery.

3. Spray the work lightly with fixative. Start to build up a contrast of cool and warm tones using blue and green in the shadow areas.

6. Overlay the colours so that the pastel strokes remain visible but the image works as a whole form. Work over the figure to heighten the tonal contrasts.

9. Round out the forms of the figure using a dark flesh pink, contrasted with cool green in the shadows. Use pinks and browns to warm the drawing.

Finished picture · blocking in using pure colour

As seen in the finished picture, it is the combination of forceful, vertical strokes used to define a largely horizontal subject which creates a harmonious, stable image.

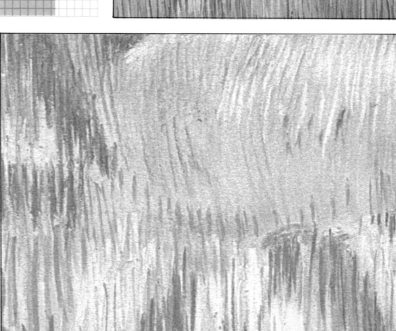

Thin lines of pure colour are laid down in directional strokes next to and on top of one another.

In the first few stages of drawing, the artist describes large areas of colour using the side of the chalk.

Pencil

THIS PICTURE is a good example of the effective use of coloured pencils in portraiture, especially when combined with the colour of the clean white surface.

Although the artist has used line to develop tonal areas, the method of drawing is similar to the classic oil painting technique of laying down colours one over another to 'mix' new colours. This requires a confident use of colour, as once put down, coloured pencils are not easily erased. This, combined with subtle or strongly directed strokes which follow or exaggerate the planes of the figure, creates a powerful image.

An interesting feature of the composition is the use of the white paper within the figure to describe the face, hands, and hair highlights. In the model's left hand, one simple line is all that is needed to separate the figure from its environment. The nearly bare areas of the face and hands are heightened by the surrounding dark area, which, in turn, plays off against the white of the paper.

Materials

Surface
White drawing paper

Size
12in × 16in (30cm × 40cm)

Colours
Dark red	Raw umber
Light green	Ultramarine blue
Magenta	Yellow ochre

Initial colour areas · dark details

In the final stages
of drawing, the
artist reworks dark
detail areas with a
strong blue pencil.

The outlines of
the figure are first
sketched in with a
warm brown. The
artist then blocks in
shadow areas with a
cool blue. Here he is
working back into
the face with light
strokes of orange to
begin to build up
flesh tones. Note the
use of loose strokes.

1. Sketch in the outline of the face in raw
umber. Use ultramarine blue for shadows
and hair and very light strokes of the same
colour in the blouse.

3. With red and yellow, put in loose
strokes to define hair tone. Strengthen
outlines of face with ultramarine blue. Put
in dark shadow area to right of face

5. Overlay magenta area with red. Create
stronger shadow areas with ultramarine
blue.

2. With pale green, begin to define shadow
areas of the face with very light hatching
and crosshatching. With dark blue, put in
the eye details.

4. Work into the hair with directional
strokes of red. Overlay light strokes of blue
and red in the blouse with loose,
scratching strokes.

6. Work back into hair with burnt umber.
Use pale green to put in highlights in the
cup.

Pen and ink

A PROFILE CAN be as successful in capturing a person's likeness as the traditional full-faced portrait because it clearly shows the contours of the individual's features. In this painting, the structure of the form is broken into a pattern of shapes by extremes of light and shadow. A strong image is constructed by using the basic techniques of hatching and stippling. The drawing uses high tonal contrasts, but note that there are no solid black areas; the darkest tones consist of layers of dense crosshatching built up in patterns of parallel lines. Details of texture and shadow in the face are stippled with the point of the nib. The vigorous activity in the drawing is offset by broad patches of plain white paper indicating the fall of light over the form.

Observe the subject carefully as you work, moving the pen swiftly over the paper. Pen strokes should be loose and lively or the result can all too easily look stiff and studied.

Materials

Surface
White HP cartridge paper

Size
10in × 11.5in (25cm × 29cm)

Tools
HB pencil
Dip pen with medium nib

Colours
Black waterproof India ink

1. Hatch in a dark tone down one side of the head to throw the profile into relief. Continue to build up detail in the face.

3. Broaden out the shadows and crosshatch areas of the background behind the head to darken the tones.

5. Draw in patches of dark tone to show folds in the clothing. Define the hairline and shape of the ear with crosshatching.

2. Work on shadows inside the shape of the head with fine parallel lines slanted across the paper. Work outwards into the background in the same way.

4. Vary the tones in the background gradually covering more of the paper. Work into the head and clothes with small, detailed patterns.

6. Work over the whole image intensifying the tones with hatching and stippling. Develop a high contrast of light and dark down the face and body.

Using paper to model the face

The initial pencil sketch of the head is used only as a reference for developing shadow and highlight areas. Note in particular how the shadows within the face and in the background create the profile of the head.

Pastel

THERE IS A long history of pastel portrait drawing and some of these drawings, with their finished surface of subtly blended colour, are nearly indistinguishable from an oil painting. In fact, the term 'pastel painting' has become as common as 'pastel drawing'. While the early pastellists most likely spent as much time on their work as a painter would on an elaborate portrait, contemporary artists have developed techniques of drawing which are flexible and less time-consuming than these early drawing methods.

The basic structure of this drawing is built upon woven lines and hatched blocks of tone using a limited range of colour. Once the fundamental shapes and tones are established, the subject is rendered with layers of bright colour.

Pastel is powdery and difficult to work with if the surface becomes too densely covered. Thus, it is worthwhile to spray the drawing with fixative frequently to keep the colour fresh and stable.

Materials

Surface
Beige pastel paper

Size
25in × 18in (62.5cm × 45cm)

Tools
Soft, large brush for blending
Pastles
Putty eraser
Fixative

Colours

Apple green	Scarlet
Black	Ultramarine blue
Light blue	Venetian red
Pink	White
Prussian blue	Yellow

1. Draw up the basic shapes of the image in Prussian blue, sketching in rough outlines and a brief indication of tones.

3. Refine details of the features with strong lines of dark blue and flesh out the face with solid blocks of white and red.

5. Block in light tones in the face with pink and pale blue. Lay in broad areas of dark tone with black and Prussian blue, working out from the figure.

7. Lay in dark background tones to emphasize the form of the figure. Overlay and blend the colours to mix the tones, working over the whole image.

2. Build up the linear and tonal structure with Venetian red, developing the loose modelling of the forms. Strengthen the drawing with fine black lines.

4. Spray the work with fixative and let it dry. Draw into the figure with blue and black correcting the outlines and adding extra details in line and tone.

6. Develop the intensity of colour, using strong, bright hues to lift the overall tone. Link vivid yellow highlights on the face with the same colour in the background.

8. Bring out the form with strong white highlights. Apply the pastel thickly and blend the colour softly with a dry brush. Strengthen light tones in the background.

Strengthening background and face with black

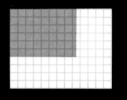

Once general shadow and highlight areas have been blocked in, the artist works back into the picture with a black pastel to develop facial details. Here he is outlining the shape of the glasses.

With a black pastel, the artist darkens the shadow area beside the face. This has the effect of forcing the flesh tones of the face to stand out in bold relief.

IN CAPTURING THE character of a subject, a quick sketch is often more successful than a carefully worked painting. The loose, vibrant colours of pastels are particularly suited for quick sketches using a vigorous, calligraphic style, as shape and texture can be shown through the activity of the colour rather than the meticulous delineation of forms.

In this drawing, pastel strokes are multidirectional and the colours warm and bright, giving an impression of a fleeting image; the model is frozen in a split second of time, not carefully posed for a long sitting. This is a quality which photographers often capture, and thus photographs are often a good source of reference material for this type of portrait.

Tonal contrasts are skilfully manipulated with black used sparingly for dark tones and outlines. Facial shadows are created with mauve and a vivid dark red, and thick white highlights give an impression of light across the face. The movement and texture of the hair is represented by heavily scribbled strokes of bright orange.

Materials

Surface
Blue-grey pastel paper

Size
11in × 15in (27.5cm × 37.5cm)

Tools
Fixative

Colours

Black	Pink
Burnt sienna	Ultramarine blue
Mauve	White
Orange	Yellow

Blending preliminary tones · highlighting the face

1. Sketch in the outline of the figure in burnt sienna. Work into the face with lines of bright orange, ultramarine and pink against dark shadows in the hair.

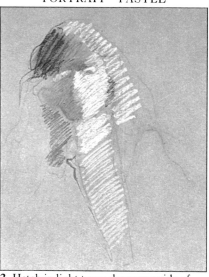

2. Hatch in light tones down one side of the figure with broad, grainy strokes of white. Move across the whole figure putting in orange, yellow and blue.

After the outlines of the head are sketched in, the artist lays in very thin strokes of warm and cool tones, blending them with his fingers.

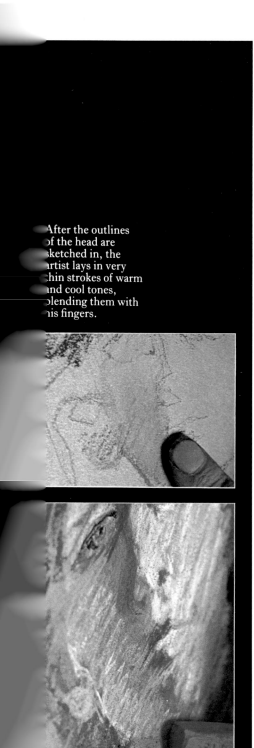

Highlighting the face with strong warm tones. Note how the artist has used strokes of pure colour in the shadow areas and how the warm oranges and pinks mix with the cool, tinted paper.

3. Accentuate the shapes in the face with fine black lines and patches of strong colour. Heighten light tones with pink and mauve against warm dark red shadows.

4. Build up the light colour in the face and work over the hair with heavy strokes of black, white and orange.

5. Outline the hand and arm with black and block in dark flesh tones with orange and mauve. Lay in a dark blue background tone.

6. Draw vigorously into all the shapes with strong colour, developing the tones and texture and highlighting the face and hand.